One More Night With The Frogs

By Jesse Duplantis

New Orleans, Louisiana

Unless otherwise indicated, all scripture quotations are taken from the *King James Version* of the Bible.

One More Night With The Frogs
ISBN 0-9728712-5-X

New Edition
Published by Jesse Duplantis Ministries
P.O. Box 20149
New Orleans, Louisiana 70141
www.jdm.org

One More Night With The Frogs

God raised up a man named Moses to deliver the children of Israel from Egyptian slavery...but it wasn't easy for him. Moses wasn't what you'd call a "born leader," and, in fact, he was one of the most unpopular pastors ever. He pastored three million people, and it seemed like nobody really liked him. Some of them wanted him dead!

Actually, Moses would have been dead had his mother not orphaned him as a baby. His childhood was weird by Hebrew standards since he was actually raised by a royal Egyptian family - the same family who ordered all the Hebrew children under two to be killed. How's that for a paradox? God works in mysterious ways. The most unlikely candidates for leadership are often the ones to whom He chooses to show His amazing power.

Moses' mother wasn't anybody's fool, and she had a plan to save her son from death. She put him in a basket by the water's edge where the Pharaoh's daughters bathed, hoping that one of them would see him, have mercy on him and raise him as their own. Sure enough, one of the women did exactly that, and Moses was raised in the house of Pharaoh.

This made him a very rich man, but all his new family's wealth and power didn't distract him from the unjust treatment happening to his people. You see, Moses knew his heritage, and the older he got, the more it bothered him to see the Hebrew people living in slavery.

Moses may have been able to see right from wrong, but he was by no means perfect. In fact, the man had a fierce temper when it came to Egyptian taskmasters, and one day, his temper drove him to commit murder.

The Bible tells us that Moses saw an Egyptian beating one of the Hebrew slaves, and it angered him so much that he immediately killed the Egyptian and buried his body. When Pharaoh heard about this, it made him furious! He sought to kill Moses as punishment for his crime against the Egyptian. But, Moses wasn't a fool, and he didn't hang around long enough to feel Pharaoh's wrath. Instead, he ran away and hid out in a town called Midian, and it was there that God began to work on Moses' character.

Moses had issues! But God saw His heart, and although his temperament was not perfect, He chose Moses to lead His people out of slavery.

Before God would put him in that position, however, he had some growing up to do. He had to work some things *out* and other things *in* to Moses' character.

Growing Out of Diapers and Into Mature Faith

God will never ask you to do something until you've worked out some of those "new-born" issues. He didn't call Moses to leadership as a newborn floating in the reeds, and He won't call baby Christians to leadership either. A firm foundation in Christ must be laid first.

You see, nobody begins life as a wise person. Everybody has physical and mental growing up to do, and we all make mistakes. It's just part of life.

When we accept Jesus as our Savior, we are "re-born" in the spirit realm, and God expects us to begin growing up spiritually. As we learn more of God's Word, His way of doing things, and develop our relationship with Him, we grow in godly wisdom. Wisdom is the characteristic we need to lead ourselves and others well.

The Bible tells us in Luke 12:48, *"For unto whomsoever much is given, of him shall be much required..."* This means that as you mature as a Christian, God will require more of you. He's not going to cut you as much slack as He first did. He's not going to treat you like a baby anymore. You're going to have to learn to rely upon His Word.

Before you accepted Jesus, you simply relied on your five senses to get through life - everything was determined by what you saw, tasted, touched, smelled and heard. Now that you're "born again," instead of relying on your basic senses, you can depend upon the Spirit of God, who lives within you, to guide your life. This is a sign of spiritual maturity.

I believe that God gets no pleasure in seeing Christians who've been saved for 40 years still wearing diapers, sucking their thumbs and whining about all the issues of life. He gets no pleasure in Christians who let the devil whip them as if they have no hope and faith. We are powerful because we have God! That gives us hope in any situation. The more we renew our mind to His ways, the more confident we should be in our faith and the more "grown-up" we should act when it comes to "doing" the Word.

Another sign of maturity is patience. James 1:4 says, *"But let patience have her perfect work, that ye may be perfect and entire, wanting nothing."* Patience is not an instinct; it's something that you learn by doing. Babies don't have it, but grown men and women of God should have it. Hebrews 6:12 says, *"That ye be not slothful, but followers of them who through faith and patience inherit the promises."*

Moses did some growing up in Midian. It was there that he married and started a family, and much time passed before he had his burning bush experience. After the Pharaoh died, the Bible tells us that God decided that it was the right time for Moses to rise up into leadership and set the children of Israel free. Notice that God is the one who chose the person to lead and the time to save the people.

As the flames on the bush roared, God called Moses to do the job. Of course, Moses didn't think he could do it. He said, *"Who am I, that I should go unto Pharaoh, and that I should bring forth the children of Israel out of Egypt?"* (Exodus 3:11). But God knew Moses, and He knew Himself! He chose the man with a heart for the job. After all, He knew that Moses just needed to be encouraged and to know that he was not alone. So God assured Moses that He would not do it alone and said, *"Certainly I will be with thee..."* (Exodus 3:12).

This is an important point for you to remember in life. If God asks you to do something, He will always help you to get it done. You may not be able to do anything worthy on your own, but with Him, ALL things are possible!

There is Always Opposition Before Freedom

Moses obeyed God and went back to Egypt, but freeing the people wasn't exactly easy. The new Pharaoh wasn't about to give up his slaves just because Moses said, "Let my people go!" But that didn't make any difference to Moses. Read the Bible and you'll see that Moses just kept on commanding the situation to change - he stuck to the same line, "Let my people go!"

Now, this is a good point, because the truth is that there is always opposition before freedom. It can be disheartening, but it is part of the process because there can be no testimony without a test. If you want results, you're going to have to stick with it. Nothing comes easy, and if it's worth something to God, the devil is going to fight it!

The Bible tells us in Exodus that Moses told Pharaoh what God would do to Egypt if he didn't free the slaves, but Pharoah didn't listen. He didn't care because he didn't believe in Moses' God. So, do you know what he did? Pharaoh made the slaves work even harder out of spite, and he ordered them to be beaten if they didn't produce more work with less materials.

This ticked the people off - at Moses! All of the unfair treatment made the children of Israel wish that Moses had never come, and they told him so. They even wished the judgment of God on him. Moses didn't know what to do! Everything was looking worse than when he started, which is an important lesson to learn about dealing with opposition.

Sometimes it can look like you're making no headway at all. You can do what God said, and things can seem worse. Remember, if God said to do it, there is a reason for you to continue. The devil is just fighting you and betting that you'll give up. Don't give in. He won't win if you keep on going.

The devil is an idiot, and he will only attack you with what is "common to man" (1 Cor. 10:13). So, it's going to be the same old attacks as usual. Remember, the Bible says that he'll crack eventually and he'll flee. But you've got to put up some resistance to his attacks (James 4:7). The Lord, on the other hand, will never crack! The God we serve is the same yesterday, today and forever, and He will always win. (Hebrews 13:8) If you stick with Him, you'll win too.

Now, back to the story: *"Then the Lord said to Moses, 'Now, you shall see what I will do to Pharaoh. For with a strong hand he will let them go, and with a strong hand he will drive them out of his land'"* (Exodus 6:1). This is God's encouragement to Moses when he was faced with the opposition.

The Devil may Mimic and Refuse to Recognize God's Power

Next, God said He would prove His presence to Pharaoh and *"...multiply My signs and My wonders in the land of Egypt...that I may lay My hand on Egypt and bring My armies and My people, the children of Israel, out of the land of Egypt by great judgments. And the Egyptians shall know that I am the Lord, when I stretch out My hand on Egypt and bring out the children of Israel from among them"* (Exodus 7:3-5).

What was God saying? Plagues are coming! Pharaoh saw the first sign when Aaron's rod was turned into a snake, but it didn't change his mind. He had his own magicians do the same thing. This is another important point.

You see, the devil can mimic the work of God. There were sorcerers, magicians and "wise men" in those days that pretended to have power. There are the same kind of people on earth today, but don't be fooled by them.

Don't let the devil's mockery of God's power

impress you. It's nothing but lies created by a loser angel who is trying to be God, but he will never be God. He's already lost, but he's so filled with his own pride that he continues to fight a losing battle.

You see, when Aaron's rod swallowed up the others rods, it was a clear sign from God. It was a miracle that Pharaoh should have noticed, but he was bent on rebellion. The devil will not always recognize the miracle of God on your life. Like the arrogant Pharaoh, he will do everything he can to dismiss the work of God. He will throw thoughts of doubt into your mind to discourage you and send people your way that will try to explain away the miracle. Don't listen to him!

Don't give in to thoughts of doubt. Turn a deaf ear to anyone who discourages you. Be like Moses, and refuse to listen to the devil!

Frogs, Frogs and More Frogs!

Some people think that God is very solemn, but the Bible shows us that He can be dramatic. Listen to this. When Pharaoh refused to let God's people go, God sent plagues to hit Egypt like they had never seen before...and I'm not talking about just a little bad weather. I'm talking about rivers filled with blood and sudden, massive infestations of insects like lice, flies and locusts!

Between the fiery hails, swarms of insects, boils on their bodies and the dead animals scattered everywhere, these were a bunch of miserable people! God was serious about proving His sovereignty and power to all of Egypt, and He used 10 big, nasty, signs and wonders to do it.

It wasn't until the last one (the death of all the first-born Egyptians) that Pharaoh had had enough, and by then, he was so desperate for normalcy that he did exactly as God said he would do - he drove the children of Israel off his land.

Now, the one plague that I haven't mentioned is the one upon which this book's title is based - the FROGS! One of the craziest things I've ever read in the Bible is Pharaoh's response to this plague. Now, this wasn't a few frogs around the palace, this was a massive infestation of "croak" and "ribbit!"

> *And the LORD spake unto Moses, Go unto Pharaoh, and say unto him, Thus saith the LORD, Let my people go, that they may serve me.*
>
> *And if thou refuse to let them go, behold,* ***I will smite all thy borders with frogs:***
>
> *And* ***the river shall bring forth frogs***

abundantly, which shall go up and come into thine house, *and* ***into thy bedchamber,*** *and* ***upon thy bed,*** *and* ***into the house of thy servants,*** *and* ***upon thy people,*** *and* ***into thine ovens,*** *and* ***into thy kneading troughs:***

And the frogs ***shall come up both on thee,*** *and* ***upon thy people,*** *and* ***upon all thy servants.***

Exodus 8:1-4

That's a lot of frogs. Think about what it would be like to have frogs in the house, frogs in the bed, frogs on the servants and frogs on the citizens! Can you imagine opening up an oven and finding frogs? Kneading dough for bread, and mixing in frogs?! The Bible says that frogs came out of the rivers, streams and ponds until they ***"...covered the land of Egypt"*** (vs. 6).

Again, Pharaoh's magicians caused frogs to come up too, but they couldn't put a stop to it. So, here is what that crazy Pharaoh said.

Then Pharaoh called for Moses and Aaron, and said, ***Entreat the LORD, that he may take away the frogs from me, and from my people; and I will let the people go,*** *that they may do sacrifice unto the LORD.*

And Moses said unto Pharaoh, Glory over me: ***when shall I entreat for thee, and for thy servants, and for thy people,***

to destroy the frogs from thee and thy houses, that they may remain in the river only?

And he said, Tomorrow*. And he said, Be it according to thy word: that thou mayest know that there is none like unto the LORD our God.*

Exodus 8:8-10

Tomorrow?! Pharaoh had a choice in the matter! He knew that Moses could remove the frogs as quickly as they appeared, but the idiot said "Tomorrow." Why? Why did Pharaoh want to spend one more night with the frogs? He was sick of those lousy, stinky frogs! The Egyptians were tormented day and night with them.

They had frogs in their beds, frogs in their kitchens, frogs everywhere they walked. Can you imagine trying to kiss your wife in the middle of the night, and kissing a big bull frog instead? The Egyptians couldn't get up to go to the bathroom without walking on frogs!

All Pharaoh had to say was, "NOW, IMMEDIATELY! I don't want to spend one more night with those stinking frogs!" Yet, when God gave Pharaoh the choice of when to be rid of them, he said, "Tomorrow."

Pharaoh had decided to spend one more night with the frogs.

Now, if you had a problem like this, wouldn't you want your problem solved at the earliest time possible? I know I would. That's why it really bothers me to see Christians putting up with problems longer than they have to!

Do *you* put up with problems sent to you by the devil longer than you need to? Do you procrastinate when it comes to your faith? Have you decided to spend "one more night with the frogs?"

Don't Put Off Your Answer Until "Tomorrow"

Maybe you're married to an unbeliever, and you're hoping that he will get saved. Maybe you need a job, and you're hoping that one will open up soon. Maybe you're sick, and you're hoping that God will heal you.

Well, let me tell you something: hoping doesn't get rid of frogs. It's faith in God that changes circumstances. It's obedience to His Word that brings results. Faith is a force, and you have to use it to see it work. It's action-oriented. Think of it like this: Hope is a good blueprint, but it's always in the future. Hope may draw up the plans, but it's faith that builds the house.

Too many people put off their answer until "tomorrow." They need God's help desperately at that moment but say "tomorrow" when God is saying, *"...behold, now is the accepted time; behold, now is the day of salvation"* (2 Cor. 6:2).

Faith is in the NOW. Unfortunately, a lot of people can't believe that something can start happening immediately. They don't realize how faith works, and so they put off receiving the answer to their prayer by "hoping" instead of "faithing."

When you "hope" that God will save your loved ones and answer all of your prayers, you're probably just wishing...and wishing doesn't get anything done. You may think that you need more faith, but the truth is, you just need to use the little bit that you've got!

Get daring with your faith in God. Get bold! Go beyond the realm of hope by stopping yourself from the typical Christian procrastination. Why put off your answer until tomorrow? Why not get into the realm of the NOW?

> *Now faith is the substance of things hoped for, the evidence of things not seen. For by it the elders obtained a good report.*
> Hebrews 11:1-2

Refuse to Spend Another Night With the Frogs.

By the words of his own mouth, Pharaoh spent one more night with the frogs. Moses gave him a choice when he said, "Be it according to thy word." You have a choice too.

Throughout the Bible, you can find references to the power of faith and the spoken word. Jesus consistently taught that we should "speak" to our problems - the waves, the wind, the mountain, or to whatever is trying to shake us up or get in our way. We have the power to command change.

If you keep saying, "It doesn't look like we'll ever do anything." You're right, you won't do anything! When you begin to study the Word, you will find out that it really doesn't matter what circumstances say. God's Word is the final authority, and when you use it in faith, it can produce miraculous change.

So, don't put off receiving your miracle until tomorrow. Never say, "Later, when God gets ready, He's going to heal me." He is ready today! Isaiah 53:5, *"But He was wounded for our transgressions, He was bruised for our iniquities: the chastisement of our peace was upon Him; and with His stripes we are healed."* Notice it says you "are" healed. That is present tense, it's a "now" concept that is baffling to the mind but completely correct in the spirit realm.

Your healing came at a high price. Jesus was innocent of all sin, and yet, He allowed them to whip His back so badly that it tore His skin until His kidneys were exposed. I don't mean to disgust you with the details, but it's something that you need to get a revelation of if you're struggling with healing. You need to know what Jesus went through for you so that you accept it. Remember, it's not what you've done that is going to bring about a healing; it's what He did on the cross. When you accept it and believe that you are healed, your body actually goes to work to heal itself. It listens to your spirit.

Jesus died innocently so that you might live eternally with God. He was chastised so that you might have peace in this life. Stripes were laid on His back so that you might receive healing for your own body, and He was made poor on the cross so that you might become rich.

Don't Let Satan Hold You Any Longer Than It Takes To Use the Name of Jesus

I get angry when the devil attacks me because I know what the blood did for me. Some people think I don't have any problems, but the devil fights me too. He doesn't like what I'm doing for God, and sometimes he tries to tell me that I'll never make it, that I'm going down and he's going to be the one to shut me down. Do you know how I respond to that? In faith and boldness!

I tell that idiot, "This is one boy you better look at good, because I'm going to chase you from the West Coast to the East Coast. I'm going to blow you away with the powerful name of Jesus!" It's my way of talking, and he gets the point.

That fool doesn't realize that I've got a direct line to the throne of Almighty God because of my relationship with Jesus. The Lord said, *"Whatsoever ye shall ask the Father in my name, He will give it to you"* (John 16:23). So, I don't let satan hold me down any longer than it takes me to use the name of Jesus. I refuse to spend another night crying over the frogs.

Satan may have been holding you in bondage to "frogs" like drug addiction, alcoholism or even overeating habits. Isn't it about time to get rid of them? You are not powerless, you know. Jesus has given you the authority over all the attacks of the devil, and if he's attacking you in a certain area of life, then it is time to put your foot down.

Take back your power. Get control over your life by making a solid decision. Don't put it off until tomorrow; use your faith and crucify your flesh today. Do it NOW! Remember, God's Word already said you could do it. Jesus gave you the power. Now, it's up to you. Your word determines the final outcome.

"Tomorrow I'll Begin My Diet"

How many times have you said that? How many times has "tomorrow" turned into next week, and the next and the next? How about stopping the cycle by starting now?

"But it's noon on Sunday," you might say. So, what! Your body will do what you tell it to do, and it can start changing its ways right now. It doesn't have to be Monday morning!

Your life will begin to change when you take the reigns and stop allowing your body to rule. Make a quality decision to begin today and stick to it. Pray to God to give you strength, and dig your heels in when it comes to your victory.

Now, you may have to rebuke the food in the name of Jesus. Even if it is pizza, and you can eat 14 of them, look at that pizza and tell your body, "You'll not have it." Your body will kick against you and say, "I want it, give it to me NOW!" Tell your body, "No! In the name of Jesus, you will not have it!" Remember that your body is a follower. It will send your mind all sorts of signals, but don't listen to self-destructive thoughts. Put down thoughts that don't agree with your plan. Don't give your body the lead position.

That's what happened to me and my diet. I'm about 5'8," and at one time I weighed 220 pounds. I didn't understand how I ever got fat! But the truth was that I was in denial! I wasn't counting the 14 gallons of gumbo and five pounds of rice. I didn't count the handfuls of snacks I ate all day long.

It seemed like somebody was always begging me to eat just one more little piece of cake. By the time I was finished, I'd eaten almost half a cake. If I ate less, I fooled myself into thinking it was alright...but less of junk food is still junk food.

For years, I made promises to God and to myself that I would lose weight "tomorrow." Finally, the Lord said, "You are lying like a dog, Jesse. You won't lose weight. You enjoy being fat." He was right. Man, every time I sat down my belly button would smile at me. I didn't like it, but not enough to quit overeating.

You see, some people make excuses for being overweight. They say, "I can't help it. My Mama is fat, my Daddy is fat and it's just natural that I'm fat." No, what's natural is every time your elbow bends your mouth opens up. You may have learned their bad habits, but I will tell you this much - if they wire your jaw, you'll die skinny. You see, there is a difference between real hunger and an indulgent appetite. Appetite says, "I believe I'll have another few pieces of pie."

I told my body, "In the name of Jesus, you are shutting down. You are losing this weight!" My body had a fit. It wanted food. I saw a dog that looked like a pot roast to me. But once I refused to spend one more night with the "frogs," I lost more than 45 pounds.

The same principle applies to smoking, drinking, lack of exercise or anything to which you are in bondage. Determine in your heart not to spend another night with that "frog." If you get weak, turn to God's Word for strength. *"And hath made us kings and priests unto God and His Father; to Him be glory and dominion for ever and ever. Amen"* (Rev. 1:6). *"I am He that liveth, and was dead; and, behold, I am alive for evermore, Amen; and have the keys of hell and of death"* (Rev. 1:18).

When the devil attacks you, tell him, "I serve Jesus Christ. He's alive and has the keys to hell, which happens to be your house, and you don't know how to change the door locks!"

Jesus' name is the most powerful name in Heaven, on the earth and in hell. When you say the name of Jesus, everything in those three places has to bow down at the name. He is King of Kings, and He lives inside of you. You've got the power to make a change now.

Never Get Accustomed to Living with the Frogs

Many years ago, my brother-in-law and I worked in the same office building together. I was using a few rooms for my ministry, and he had a law practice. His secretary was a very mild-mannered woman, but one day in particular I remember her taking a stand against her "frogs." She decided that she was not going to be accustomed to living with it.

Her husband was a welder and steady work was hard to find. So, she began to diligently pray for him to get more work - she began to apply her faith for it and act on it by consistently speaking the end result. God blessed them so much that her husband asked her not to pray so hard! He got so much work, he didn't have any time at home. What happened? She had decided to believe God's Word. She refused to get accustomed to those circumstances of lack sent by satan.

Many people have accepted the "frogs" sent to them by satan and even made them little pets. For them, things such as constant financial problems, family problems or health problems have become a way of life. But, we must never get accustomed to the circumstances sent by satan. We must only receive the kingship privileges of the Almighty God given through Jesus' name.

"Jesus said unto him, If thou canst believe, ***all things are possible to him that believeth****"* (Mark 9:23). Don't deny the problem exists; just deny its right to touch you because you are a born-again, Spirit-filled believer.

Once you get accustomed to circumstances like cursing, drinking, adultery, violence, etc., you will live with them the rest of your life. That may be a common way to live, but it's not "normal" to God. There is a better way to live - the life of faith.

Fight the good fight of faith whenever the devil tries to hinder God's Word from coming to pass. Remember that the most powerful force in the world is faith in God's Word. It will keep you from spending one more night with the frogs. People may call you crazy, over balanced or nuts. But if you'll stand on the Word of God, your day of deliverance will come.

Your miracle will come to pass because God can't deny Himself. The Bible says, *"If we believe not, yet he abideth faithful: he cannot deny himself"* (2 Timothy 2:13). God is faithful.

You may be bound by spiritual, physical or financial problems, and those burdensome issues may be preventing you from being the person you want to be...the person God knows you can be. Know this: God doesn't want you in bondage to anyone or anything! He always has a plan to deliver His children.

Choose freedom today. Don't spend another night with sin, sickness or depression when freedom from these things is your blood-bought right. God has sent a deliverer, and His name is Jesus Christ. If you will turn to Him and obey His instruction, He will lead you out of the land of bondage.

He will remove the shackles of your slavery to that "frog" and guide your feet to the promised land. Your destiny is freedom - a life of love, joy, peace and "overflow" blessings. That's the kind of God we serve! Turn to Him today, and get the strength you need to say, "No! I will not spend one more night with these frogs!"

Prayer of Salvation

If you don't know Jesus as your personal Lord and Savior, I'd like to take this opportunity to pray with you. All God asks is for you to come to Him with a sincere heart and accept His plan of salvation through Jesus Christ. Right now, go to Him in prayer. Speak from your heart. The Bible says in Romans 10:9-10 that if you believe on the Lord Jesus Christ with your heart and confess it with your mouth, you will be saved. Your sins will be washed away when you accept what Jesus did for you. Pray this prayer right now:

"Lord Jesus, come into my life. Forgive me of all my sins. I believe that you are the Son of God and that you died on the cross and rose from the dead to make a way for me. Thank you for loving me enough to die for me, for thinking that I was worth it. Today, I accept you into my heart and give myself totally to you. I'm tired of living my own way, and I want to live your way. I need your help. Lord, create a clean heart in me right now and guide me from now on. I love you, Jesus, and I accept you as my Savior. You are now the Lord of my life!"

If you just prayed this prayer, Congratulations! You're starting a new life! 2 Corinthians 5:17 says when you accept Jesus as your savior, *"Old things are passed away; behold, all things are become new."*

Friend, you have a whole new way of life to look forward to. You've been given a clean slate – you are righteous now because of what Jesus did, and nobody can take that away! You're saved and starting a brand new life in Christ.

Please write to my ministry and let us know of your decision so that we can bless you with some more information and pray for you. God bless you as you start your new life with God today.

For a free catalog of other books and tapes by Jesse Duplantis or for information about JDM, call or write:

Jesse Duplantis Ministries
P.O. Box 20149
New Orleans, LA 70141
985.764.2000 Fax 985.764.0044
or
Visit us online at:
www.jdm.org

Look for these other books by
Jesse Duplantis

Wanting a God You Can Talk To
Also available in Braille

Jambalaya for the Soul
Also available in Braille

Breaking the Power of Natural Law
Also available in Braille

God Is Not Enough, He's Too Much
Also available in Braille

Heaven: Close Encounters of the God Kind
Also available in Braille or Spanish

What In Hell Do You Want?

Jesse's Mini-books

Don't Be Affected by The World's Message

The Battle of Life

Running Toward Your Giant

Keep Your Foot on The Devil's Neck

One More Night With The Frogs

Leave It In The Hands of A Specialist